The Hidden World of

BACTERIA

Multiplying Mixed Numbers

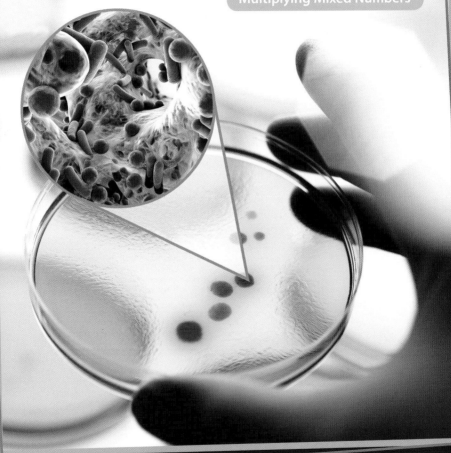

Georgia Beth

Consultants

Lisa Ellick, M.A.
Math Specialist
Norfolk Public Schools

Pamela Estrada, M.S. Ed.
Teacher
Westminster School District

Publishing Credits

Rachelle Cracchiolo, M.S.Ed., *Publisher*
Conni Medina, M.A.Ed., *Managing Editor*
Dona Herweck Rice, *Series Developer*
Emily R. Smith, M.A.Ed., *Series Developer*
Diana Kenney, M.A.Ed., NBCT, *Content Director*
Stacy Monsman, M.A., *Editor*
Kristy Stark, M.A.Ed., *Editor*
Kevin Panter, *Graphic Designer*

Image Credits: Front cover, p.1 Andrew Brookes/Getty Images; p.1 Andrew Brookes/Getty Images; p.5 Peter Horree/Alamy; p.6 The Print Collector/Alamy; p.7 (both) Wellcome Images/Science Source; p.8 Scott Camazine/Science Source; p.11 Bruce Fox University of Michigan/KRT/Newscom; p.12 (top) Aquascopic/Alamy; p.20 (top) McComas/MCT/Newscom; p.24 Courtesy, Japan Advanced Institute of Science and Technology; p.27 (both) Courtesy of Suzanne Lee, BioCouture™; all other images from iStock and/or Shutterstock.

Teacher Created Materials

5301 Oceanus Drive
Huntington Beach, CA 92649-1030
http://www.tcmpub.com

ISBN 978-1-4258-5816-2

Table of Contents

A Microscopic Mystery

Bacteria are invisible to the human eye. But, they are all around! The world is crawling with over five nonillion (noh-NIL-yuhn) of them. What does that number look like? It is the digit 5 followed by 30 zeros! There's no question that these microscopic creatures have taken over Earth.

Bacteria are one-celled organisms. They are found everywhere. They live underground. They live in human bodies. Bacteria are even strong enough to live deep in the sea. Some types of bacteria have **adapted** to cold temperatures. They can be found in the frozen tundra.

Every person on Earth is covered with bacteria. They can be found on skin and on hair. They live in people's digestive systems, too. They can even affect a person's mood or weight.

Bacteria were first discovered in the late 1600s by Antonie van Leeuwenhoek (AN-tuh-nee vahn LAY-vuhn-huhk). He observed bacteria under a microscope. He took notes about what he saw. He recorded their sizes and shapes. But, he was only just beginning to understand their secrets.

Antonie van Leeuwenhoek

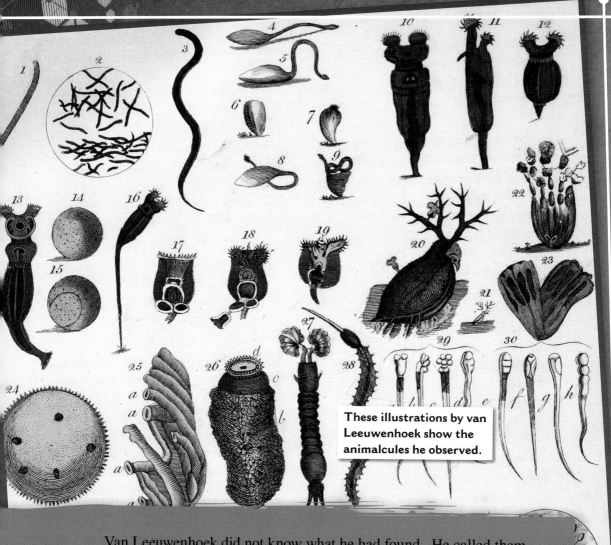

These illustrations by van Leeuwenhoek show the animalcules he observed.

Van Leeuwenhoek did not know what he had found. He called them "very little animalcules." He compared samples of **microbes** from rainwater, saliva, and other sources.

Today, people know that bacteria are 0.2 to 10 microns wide. That means they are less than $\frac{1}{100}$th of an inch (0.2 millimeters)! They can only be seen with certain magnifying glasses. The lenses magnify bacteria 300 to 1,000 times their actual size. This makes a cell that is smaller than a dot look as big as a word on this page!

The lenses van Leeuwenhoek used have confused experts. He did not have the powerful lenses that scientists have today. They believe that his lenses would have enhanced **cells** only 50 to 300 times their size. So, experts think he used something else. But, they are not exactly sure what that was. He kept his method a secret, which he took with him when he died at age 90. Van Leeuwenhoek never told anyone how he made his lenses. His techniques are still a mystery. But, scientists can gather information from the lenses themselves and through his written journals.

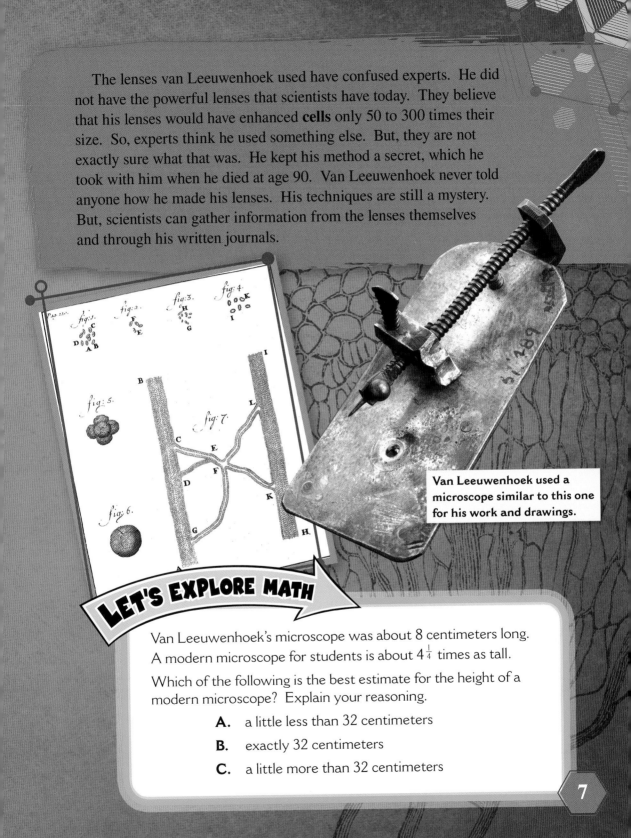

Van Leeuwenhoek used a microscope similar to this one for his work and drawings.

LET'S EXPLORE MATH

Van Leeuwenhoek's microscope was about 8 centimeters long. A modern microscope for students is about $4\frac{1}{4}$ times as tall.

Which of the following is the best estimate for the height of a modern microscope? Explain your reasoning.

    A.   a little less than 32 centimeters

    B.   exactly 32 centimeters

    C.   a little more than 32 centimeters

Bacteria Cell

Bacteria are one of the oldest life forms on Earth. Bacteria fossils have been found in rocks. These fossils date back 419.2 million to 358.9 million years. Scientists think that some bacteria have survived over 3 billion years.

Form and Function

In just one cell, bacteria have what they need to live and grow. Most have a spherical, rodlike, or spiral shape. Many have long thin tails called flagella (fluh-JEL-luh). They help the cell move. A membrane holds the cell together. Ribosomes produce proteins that fuel the cells so they can function. Like all life, bacteria have **DNA**. DNA is the material that contains all of the information about how a particular living thing looks and functions. But unlike other life forms, bacterial DNA isn't stored in a **nucleus**. Instead, it's found throughout the cell.

Most bacteria use **binary fission** to reproduce. A single cell grows until it is large enough to split into two identical daughter cells.

The process of dividing cells continues. Two cells split into 4 cells. Soon 4 cells become 8, and 8 cells become 16. This continues until there are countless cells.

This photo, taken with a microscope, shows a bacterial cell splitting into two cells during binary fission.

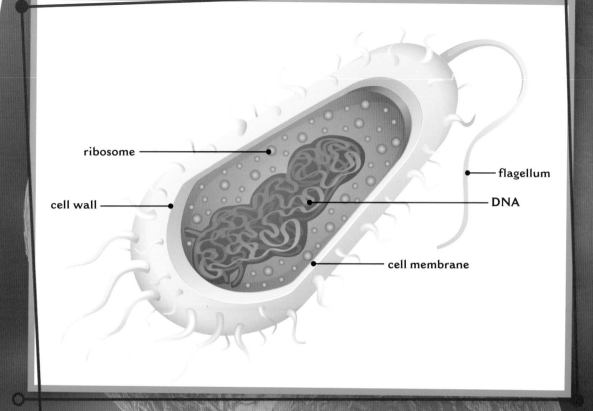

ribosome

flagellum

DNA

cell wall

cell membrane

LET'S EXPLORE MATH

Flagella can be longer than their bacteria cells. But, flagella and bacteria are still so small they are measured in *micrometers*. This is a unit of measurement equal to one-millionth of a meter!

Suppose a bacteria cell is 10 micrometers long. Its flagellum is $2\frac{1}{2}$ times as long. How long is the flagellum? Complete the strategy shown.

$10 \times 2\frac{1}{2} = (10 \times$ _____ $) + ($ _____ $\times \frac{1}{2})$

$=$ _____ $+$ _____

$=$ _____ micrometers

Bacteria's ability to quickly copy themselves helps them **evolve** over time. Strong bacteria can reproduce faster. They can adapt at a faster rate. When needed, they can adapt to changes in temperature, food, and more. Strong bacteria can survive these changes.

Biologist Richard Lenski has studied bacteria for over 25 years. In 1988, Lenski put the same *E. coli* bacteria into 12 glass flasks. Those groups began feeding and dividing. Since 1988, the 12 groups have made 50,000 **generations** of bacteria! Each group is stronger than the last. Lenski wants to find out if they will ever get strong enough that they no longer change. Their rate of change seems to be slowing down. But, they are not stopping.

But, there are times when it is not helpful to grow quickly. Some species of bacteria live deep under the ground. It is hard to live there. So, growth rates are much slower. Cells may reproduce once every few thousand years. Bacteria find ways to adapt no matter where they live.

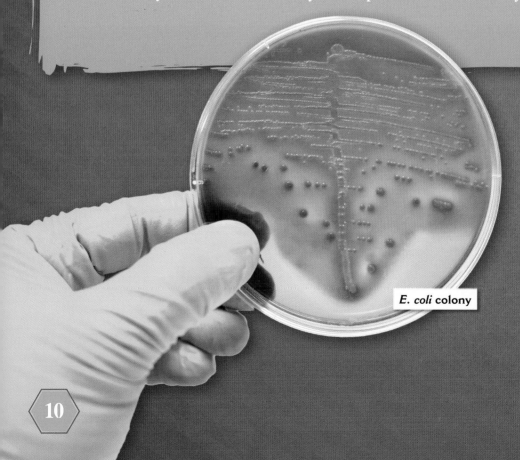

E. coli **colony**

Richard Lenski

Lenski measured the volume of E. coli samples using femtoliters, which are very small fractions of a liter.

Suppose that the volume of the first sample was about $\frac{4}{10}$ of a femtoliter. By the ten-thousandth generation, it increased its volume by $2\frac{3}{4}$ times. What is the volume of the ten-thousandth generation? Complete the area model and equations to solve the problem.

	2	+	$\frac{3}{4}$
$\frac{4}{10}$	$\frac{4}{10} \times 2 =$ ___		$\frac{4}{10} \times \frac{3}{4} =$ ___

11

Bacteria are causing this sunken ship to corrode.

Bacteria develop different colors based on water temperature, as seen here at Yellowstone National Park.

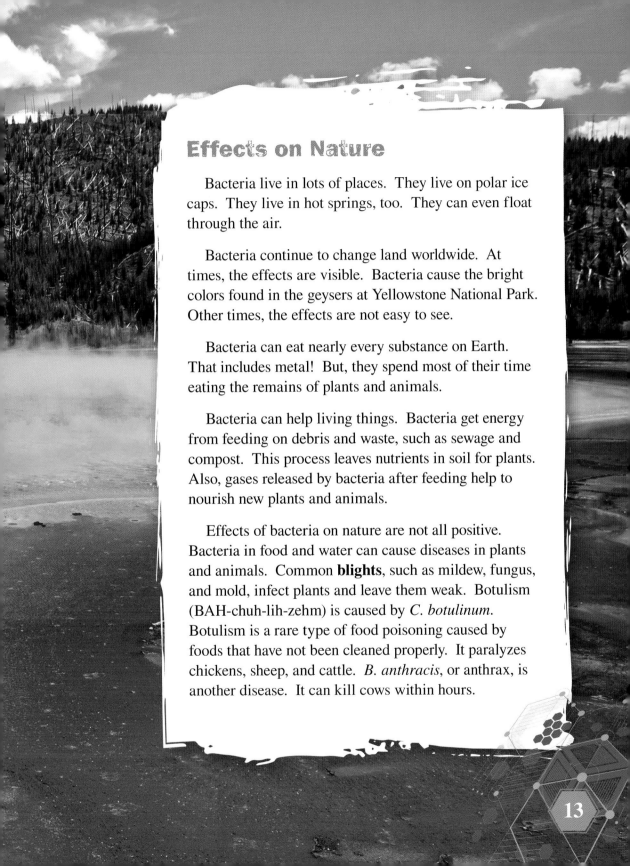

Effects on Nature

Bacteria live in lots of places. They live on polar ice caps. They live in hot springs, too. They can even float through the air.

Bacteria continue to change land worldwide. At times, the effects are visible. Bacteria cause the bright colors found in the geysers at Yellowstone National Park. Other times, the effects are not easy to see.

Bacteria can eat nearly every substance on Earth. That includes metal! But, they spend most of their time eating the remains of plants and animals.

Bacteria can help living things. Bacteria get energy from feeding on debris and waste, such as sewage and compost. This process leaves nutrients in soil for plants. Also, gases released by bacteria after feeding help to nourish new plants and animals.

Effects of bacteria on nature are not all positive. Bacteria in food and water can cause diseases in plants and animals. Common **blights**, such as mildew, fungus, and mold, infect plants and leave them weak. Botulism (BAH-chuh-lih-zehm) is caused by *C. botulinum*. Botulism is a rare type of food poisoning caused by foods that have not been cleaned properly. It paralyzes chickens, sheep, and cattle. *B. anthracis*, or anthrax, is another disease. It can kill cows within hours.

Bacteria's Effects on Humans

Bacteria can make people sick. One common example of this is salmonella. This strain of bacteria causes food poisoning. People can get it by eating raw meat, eggs, milk, or poultry. When infected, people can be ill for two to seven days. Other bacteria can cause a lot of pain. *H. pylori* forms sores in the stomach. These are called ulcers. Ulcers can be very painful.

Infections like these are treated by **antibiotics**. This medicine is made from microbes. The microbes work to fight and kill bacteria. Only doctors can prescribe this treatment. With proper use, patients can be healed.

But antibiotics do not always work. Antibiotics will not help if a **virus** causes the illness. This is because viruses and bacteria are two different things. Also, antibiotics may kill good bacteria. These help the body fight off infection. Without enough of them, bad bacteria are still able to grow. So, the infection keeps spreading.

Bacteria find ways to fight off antibiotics, too. Superbugs are strong bacteria. They have grown resistant to antibiotics. This makes them hard to kill. People can die from superbugs that cannot be treated.

H. pylori

This *H. pylori* test shows that a sample tested positive for infection.

H. pylori

C T

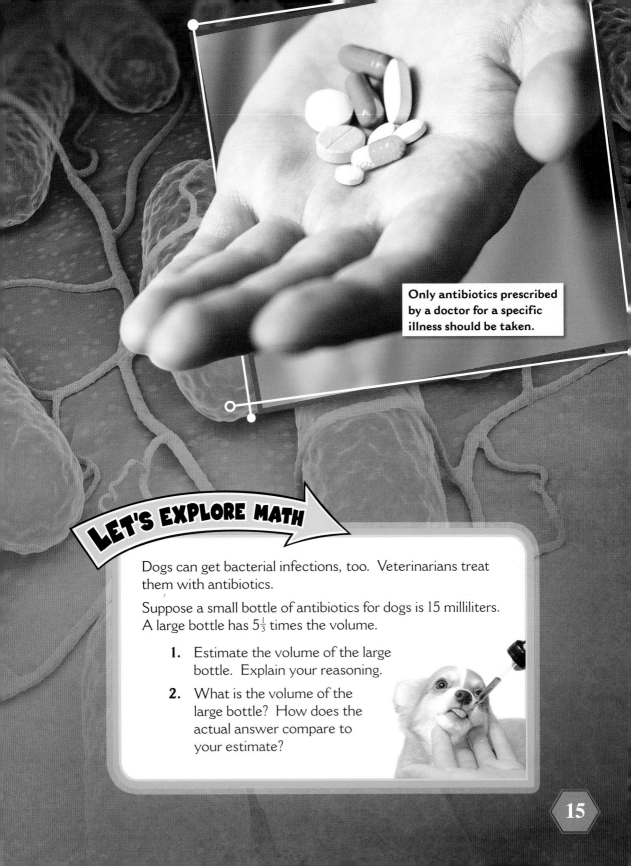

Only antibiotics prescribed by a doctor for a specific illness should be taken.

LET'S EXPLORE MATH

Dogs can get bacterial infections, too. Veterinarians treat them with antibiotics.

Suppose a small bottle of antibiotics for dogs is 15 milliliters. A large bottle has $5\frac{1}{3}$ times the volume.

1. Estimate the volume of the large bottle. Explain your reasoning.

2. What is the volume of the large bottle? How does the actual answer compare to your estimate?

It is impossible to rid bodies of all bacteria. It would actually be a bad idea! Bacteria help bodies, too.

There are lots of microbes in bodies. They create a **microbiome** in each person. Everyone has a different mix of microbes. They live in organs and cells. The mix of microbes is a balance. Big changes can happen from adding or subtracting these microbes.

Bacteria play a big role in gut health. *Gut* is another name for the stomach or abdomen. In people's guts, there are more than 1,000 species of bacteria that help digest food. They can make people gain or lose weight. Bacteria in the gut can even affect things that seem unrelated, such as seasonal allergies. Gut health is also closely tied to the health of the entire **immune system**. The American Gut Project wants to find out how microbiomes vary from person to person. They study how microbiomes and health are related.

microbes

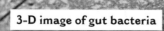
3-D image of gut bacteria

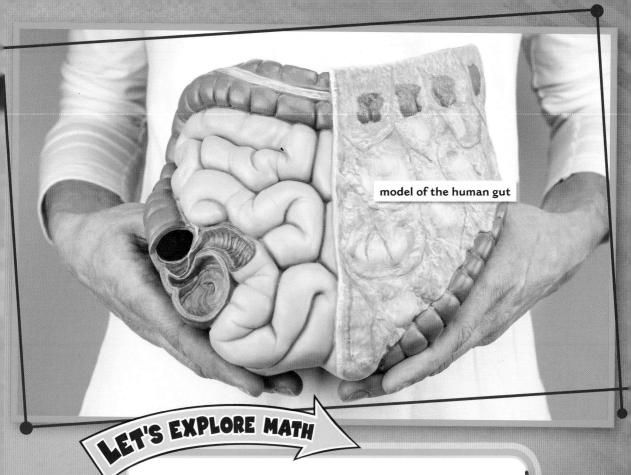

model of the human gut

LET'S EXPLORE MATH

Suppose a microbiologist at the American Gut Project is analyzing microbes in some samples. On Monday, she spends $1\frac{1}{2}$ hours in the lab. On Tuesday, she spends $2\frac{1}{2}$ times as long in the lab.

1. How many hours does she spend in the lab on Tuesday? Complete the area model and equations to solve the problem.

	2	+	$\frac{1}{2}$
1	$1 \times 2 =$ __		$1 \times \frac{1}{2} =$ __
+ $\frac{1}{2}$	$\frac{1}{2} \times 2 =$ __		$\frac{1}{2} \times \frac{1}{2} =$ __

2. How many hours does she spend in the lab on both days?

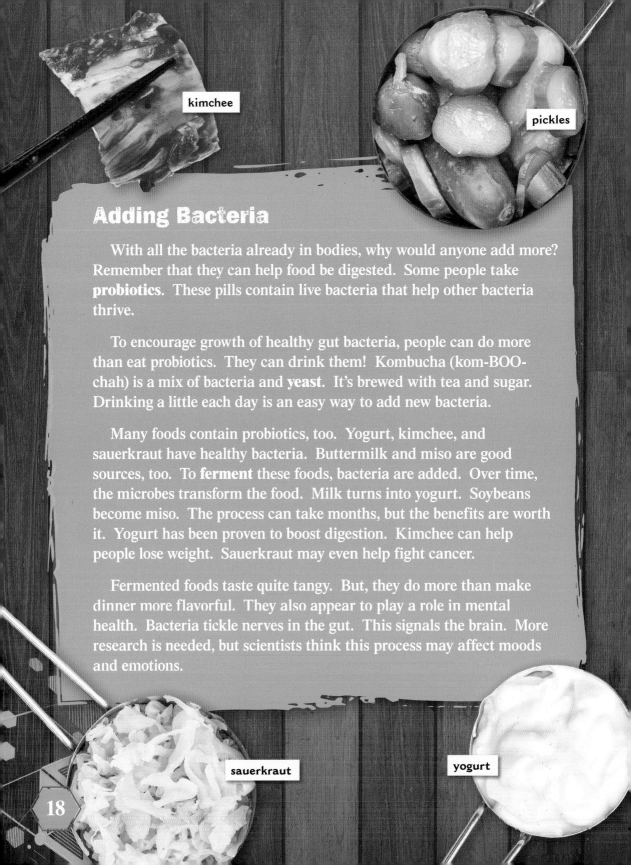

kimchee

pickles

Adding Bacteria

With all the bacteria already in bodies, why would anyone add more? Remember that they can help food be digested. Some people take **probiotics**. These pills contain live bacteria that help other bacteria thrive.

To encourage growth of healthy gut bacteria, people can do more than eat probiotics. They can drink them! Kombucha (kom-BOO-chah) is a mix of bacteria and **yeast**. It's brewed with tea and sugar. Drinking a little each day is an easy way to add new bacteria.

Many foods contain probiotics, too. Yogurt, kimchee, and sauerkraut have healthy bacteria. Buttermilk and miso are good sources, too. To **ferment** these foods, bacteria are added. Over time, the microbes transform the food. Milk turns into yogurt. Soybeans become miso. The process can take months, but the benefits are worth it. Yogurt has been proven to boost digestion. Kimchee can help people lose weight. Sauerkraut may even help fight cancer.

Fermented foods taste quite tangy. But, they do more than make dinner more flavorful. They also appear to play a role in mental health. Bacteria tickle nerves in the gut. This signals the brain. More research is needed, but scientists think this process may affect moods and emotions.

sauerkraut

yogurt

This recipe makes 1 gallon of kombucha. How much of each ingredient is needed to make 3 gallons?

$3\frac{1}{2}$ quarts water

$\frac{1}{2}$ cup sugar

$2\frac{3}{4}$ tablespoons of loose tea

2 cups of store-bought kombucha (this will add bacteria into the mixture)

1 scoby (a special blend of yeast and bacteria)

Microbes build slick, protective layer

Bacteria and other microscopic organisms can organize themselves into a thin layer — a biofilm — held together and protected by a dense, slimy chemical coating.

a staphylococcus bacteria biofilm

How a biofilm forms

1 Microbes attach to surface, adhere strongly.

2 Microbes form mushroom-like structures and produce slick sugar-protein coating.

3 Interior channels carry water, and nutrients to microbes.

4 Cells break free and spread biofilm.

Algae is a biofilm that forms in moisture-rich environments.

Biofilms

Around the world, bacteria are waging war with each other. The toughest strains destroy everything in their path. Others push rivals aside. Only the strongest survive. This is more than microscopic drama. It affects humans, too. Scientists think that studying these wars may help to create new antibiotics. Learning which bacteria can kill others may be key. They could use this knowledge to design medicine that treats superbugs.

But, bacteria do not always battle. Some types form **colonies** that grow together. Thin layers of these colonies are called biofilms. Tartar on teeth is a type of biofilm. The slime on a rock at the beach is, too. In a biofilm, bacteria on top can reach nutrients that feed the colony. They can also be easily attacked. Bacteria below are protected. But, they need help to get food. So, cells on the bottom release a chemical that top cells need to grow stronger. In return, cells share nutrients. This relationship helps all bacteria live longer.

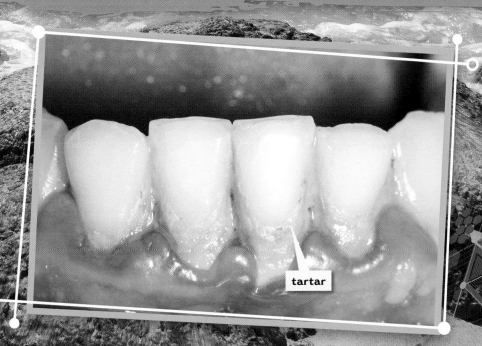

tartar

Another place biofilm may form is on skin wounds. Skin naturally has bacteria that give it nutrients. Sometimes, this bacteria or bacteria from daily life can enter cuts and scrapes. Usually, the body is able to destroy bacteria on its own. Then, the body heals. But too much bacteria can attach to the wound. When this happens, biofilm develops. Biofilms on skin wounds delay the healing process. These wounds can become very infected.

Biofilms grow by a process called **quorum** sensing. A quorum is the smallest number of members needed to do something. If there are only a few bacteria cells, not many will grow. If there are more cells, even more start growing. So, how do bacteria cells know when to grow? A few signaling molecules break away from the first bacteria that entered the wound. They explore the area. Then, they use cell-to-cell communication. This means they share information, such as the number of cells. If there are enough, infection spreads.

As biofilms grow, they get more dangerous. They become resistant to antibiotics. It is also harder for the body to fight back. This makes biofilm tough to treat. Doctors are studying how to stop this process. Their hope is to stop biofilms before they ever form.

Biofilm Development on a Skin Wound

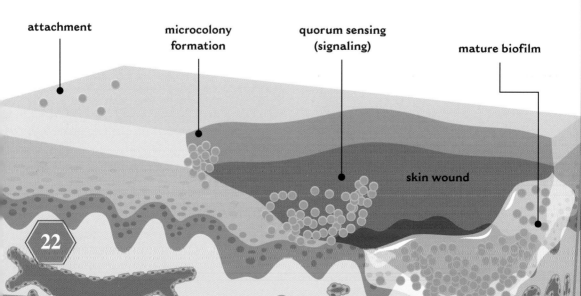

attachment

microcolony formation

quorum sensing (signaling)

mature biofilm

skin wound

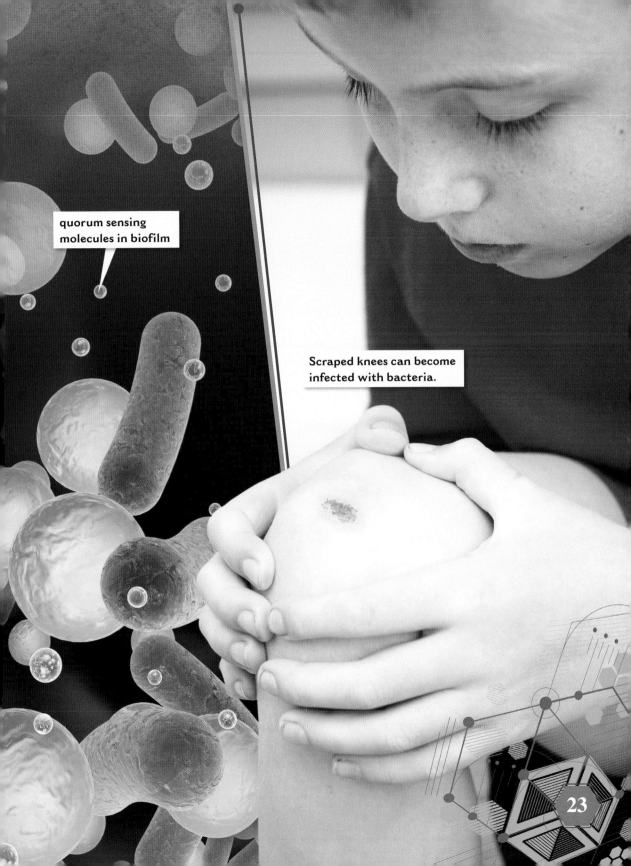

quorum sensing molecules in biofilm

Scraped knees can become infected with bacteria.

The Future of Microbiology

Scientists have learned a lot in the last 400 years since bacteria was first discovered. Today, bacteria are studied by more than doctors and scientists. Engineers want to use bacteria to solve problems. Designers want to use them, too.

One such plan is a bacteria energy farm. People want to place bacteria in liquid and use their movements to turn small **rotors**. The hope is that they will work in the same way that wind powers windmills. Rotors would then make electricity.

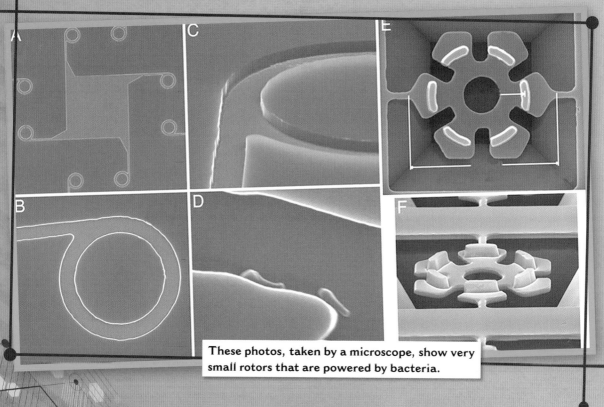

These photos, taken by a microscope, show very small rotors that are powered by bacteria.

As water enters cracks in the concrete, bacteria are stimulated to grow and seal the gap.

Another plan is to have bacteria repair sidewalks. Most sidewalks crack from pressure and harsh weather. A biologist is designing new concrete mixed with bacteria. This is called bioconcrete. When a crack forms in a sidewalk, water seeps in. The water activates the bacteria. Then, the bacteria make a substance that fills the cracks—no roadwork required!

A design firm in New York has an idea for making chairs from bacteria. It uses the materials cells produce and patterns they make as they move. This is more than a neat idea. It could be a good way to save oil, plastic, and other resources.

Van Leeuwenhoek was the first person to draw pictures of bacteria. Since then, the shapes, colors, and diversity of these cells have inspired artists. Suzanne Lee is one of those artists. She is testing bacteria to make a fabric that feels like leather. She has sewn a jacket and a dress using this fabric.

Artist Sarah Berman uses bacteria to make paint. She learned that some strains glow with a special light. So, she started growing her own bacteria. She added proteins to a safe strain of *E. coli*. After seeing the bright neon colors, she wanted to make more. She mixed cells to make different colors. While she has created great works of art, there is one downside—the color disappears once the bacteria die.

The hidden world of bacteria is more colorful than we ever imagined. The true beauty of these creatures is the way they have survived for millions of years. They have changed and grown. There is no doubt that bacteria have left their mark on the world.

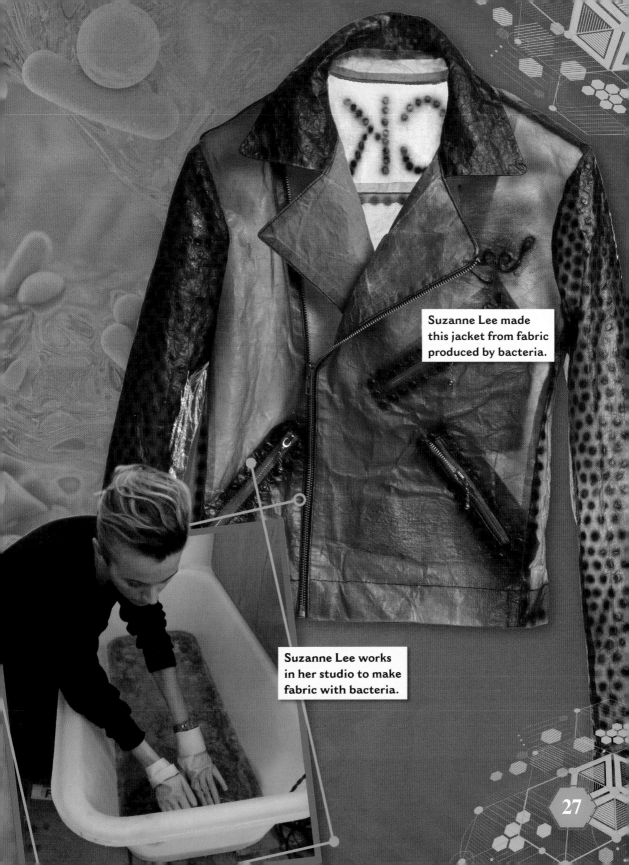

Suzanne Lee made this jacket from fabric produced by bacteria.

Suzanne Lee works in her studio to make fabric with bacteria.

⚙️ Problem Solving

Pickling is not only for cucumbers! Almost any fresh vegetable can be pickled. This process extends the amount of time foods can be stored, allows good bacteria to grow, and stops growth of bad bacteria that causes foods to spoil. Plus, it gives foods a tart, tangy flavor.

The pickling process begins by submerging foods in brine. This is water with pickling salt dissolved in it. Brine for different foods requires different amounts of pickling salt. Show that you are a pickling professional! Use the recipe for half-sour pickle brine to answer the questions.

1. The amount of pickling salt to make half-sour pickles is enough for 1 pound of cucumbers. How much salt is needed for 2 pounds of cucumbers?

2. Pickled pepper brine needs $1\frac{1}{2}$ times as much salt as brine for half-sour pickles. How much salt is needed for pepper brine?

3. Sauerkraut brine needs $\frac{2}{5}$ as much salt as half-sour brine. How much salt is needed for this brine?

4. Olives are made with full-strength brine. This brine has $2\frac{1}{4}$ times as much salt as the brine for half-sour pickles. How much salt is needed for full-strength brine?

5. How much more salt is in full-strength brine than half-sour pickle brine?

Half-Sour Pickle Brine

$\frac{3}{4}$ ounces pickling salt

2 cups water

dill, garlic, peppercorns

Glossary

adapted—changed over time

antibiotics—medicines that fight infection

binary fission—the process when a cell creates a new cell by dividing into two

blights—organisms that cause diseases in plants

cells—the smallest structures of an organism that are alive

colonies—groups of microbes, plants, or animals that grow in a particular place and belong to one species

DNA—deoxyribonucleic acid; the genetic material stored in a cell's nucleus

evolve—to change gradually

ferment—to change sugar to carbon dioxide and alcohol through a process involving yeast

generations—all of the offspring at the same stage descended from a common ancestor

immune system—the system in the body that fights illness and disease

microbes—tiny lifeforms, especially bacteria that cause diseases

microbiome—microorganisms in a particular place

nucleus—the center of a cell that contains genetic material

probiotics—types of bacteria used to help good bacteria grow or thrive in the digestive tract

quorum—the number of members that must be present for an action to be carried out

rotors—parts of a machine that turn

virus—an infectious, nonliving agent that causes diseases

yeast—any of various single-celled fungi

Index

Answer Key

Let's Explore Math

page 7:

C; Explanations will vary but may include that $8 \times 4 = 32$, so $8 \times 4\frac{1}{4}$ must be greater than 32.

page 9:

25 micrometers; 2; 10; 20; 5

page 11:

$1\frac{1}{10}$ femtoliters or equivalent: $\frac{8}{10} + \frac{12}{40}$ or $\frac{32}{40} + \frac{12}{40} = \frac{44}{40}$

	2	$+$	$\frac{3}{4}$
$\frac{4}{10}$	$\frac{4}{10} \times 2 = \frac{8}{10}$		$\frac{4}{10} \times \frac{3}{4} = \frac{12}{40}$

page 15:

1. Accept reasonable estimates and explanations. Example: *The volume of the large bottle is a little more than 75 milliliters because 15×5 is 75. I rounded $5\frac{1}{3}$ to 5, so I know the actual answer must be a little more than 75.*

2. 80 milliliters; Comparisons will vary. Example: *My estimate is a little less than the actual answer because I rounded $5\frac{1}{3}$ to 5.*

page 17:

1. $3\frac{3}{4}$ or equivalent; $2 + 1 + \frac{1}{2} + \frac{1}{4} = 3\frac{3}{4}$

	2	$+$	$\frac{1}{2}$
1	$1 \times 2 = 2$		$1 \times \frac{1}{2} = \frac{1}{2}$
$+$ $\frac{1}{2}$	$\frac{1}{2} \times 2 = \frac{2}{2} = 1$		$\frac{1}{2} \times \frac{1}{2} = \frac{1}{4}$

2. $5\frac{1}{4}$ or equivalent

page 19:

$10\frac{1}{2}$ quarts water; $1\frac{1}{2}$ cups sugar; $8\frac{1}{4}$ tablespoons loose tea; 6 cups store-bought kombucha; 3 scobies

Problem Solving

1. $1\frac{1}{2}$ ounces or equivalent
2. $1\frac{1}{8}$ ounces or equivalent
3. $\frac{3}{10}$ ounces or equivalent
4. $1\frac{11}{16}$ ounces or equivalent
5. $\frac{15}{16}$ ounces or equivalent